THE RAILWAY PAINTING
OF TERENCE CUNEO

TWEED MOUTH
YARDS

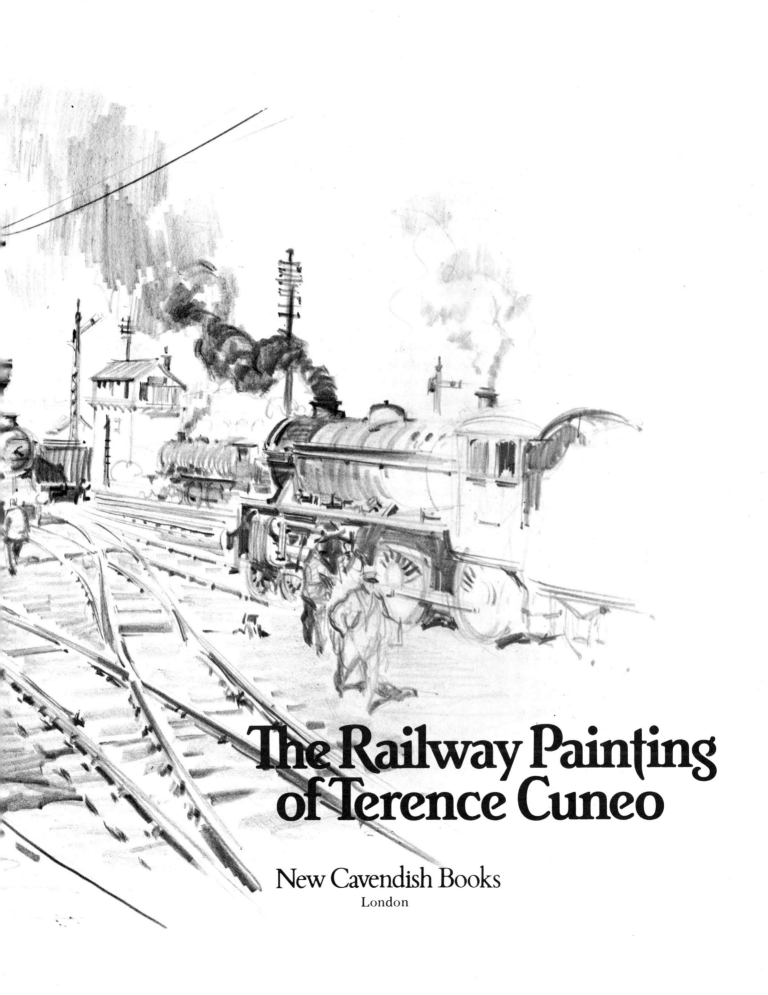

The Railway Painting of Terence Cuneo

New Cavendish Books

London

To the late Don Faulkner, PRO Southern Region, Waterloo.
A true friend and counsellor both to me and to many another
aspiring poster artist of the halcyon '60s.

First edition published in Great Britain
by New Cavendish Books – 1984

Design – John B. Cooper
Production and supervision – Narisa Levy
Editorial direction – Allen Levy

Setting and monochrome illustrations, Wyvern Typesetting Ltd, Bristol.
Colour separation, Aragorn Colour Reproduction, London.
Printed and bound by Robert Hartnoll Ltd, Bodmin

New Cavendish Books, 23 Craven Hill, London W2 3EN
Distribution: ABP, North Way, Andover, Hampshire SP10 5BE

ISBN 0 904568 43 1

Coming into King's Cross.
(Sketched from a diesel.)

Foreword

by Viscount Garnock R.S.A., B.A.

Artists depend on talent encouraged by individual taste built up over a long period of time. Seldom can any artist depict such a diversity of interest and subjects on canvas as Terence Cuneo, a painter of immensely varied ability, always with a splendid sense of humour, infectious enthusiasm, an eye for the unusual and an original frame of mind. On a topical note, Cuneo, ever generous presented to the Army Benevolent Fund a portrait he made of the wounded 'Sefton', one of the horses injured in the Hyde Park bomb outrage. This work was auctioned in September 1982 in the presence of Princess Anne, and raised £13,000 for the Fund.

In his long and distinguished career, Cuneo has painted everything from military ceremonial and battle scenes to State occasions, City Livery dinners and delightful landscapes. These works have been well represented in his earlier book *The Mouse and His Master*, but it was rightly felt that his extremely evocative railway paintings merited a book in their own right.

Whenever the name of Terence Cuneo is mentioned, whether this be amongst devotees of portrait painting, city dinners, steam enthusiasts or lovers of Victoriana, the reaction is invariably the same. It is not whether or not the subject of a particular portrait is more lifelike than that by another artist, but it is admiration and wonder at the realism of his railway scenes. It is as if one was standing alongside the running line, the smell of carbon in the nostrils, soot in the hair, a smut in one eye and a liberal all-over damp sprinkling from the cylinder drain cocks or injector overflow pipe, the whole dominated by the roar of exhaust and deafened by steam from the safety-valve. Cuneo has the special gift and talent to make the onlooker himself feel part of those memorable scenes. . .

Often one hears the question asked as to how it is that he achieves effects that are as real as they are dramatic. In the pages of this book Terry Cuneo tells the absorbing and fascinating story of the need to experience realism to create realism.

Realism is not achieved by sitting in a studio surrounded by photographs. Recipe for success is brought about by painstaking on-the-spot sketching on a trial and error basis regardless of adverse weather, darkness, or the effect of coal dust on sketches already distorted by the lurching of a poorly sprung locomotive and not without considerable danger to life and limb.

These heart-stopping experiences include a battle with the elements on the cat-walk above the Forth Bridge in a late autumn gale; coming within a hairsbreadth of being run down in a smoke-filled tunnel on the East Coast main line; and stumbling over the maze of tracks and turnouts in the ever increasing darkness outside Euston.

Why does the steam engine number such a following, command such loyalty and demand such detail and accuracy from those who portray it to the benefit and delight of the rest of us?

For many of us the romance of steam came at an early age. There was a time in my boyhood when I spent holidays within sight and sound of the West Highland line on its long climb out of Crianlarich up through Tyndrum to County March Summit and on to Rannoch Moor. Never before or since have I heard the like of the locomotive's whistle as it struggled uphill, the frosty evening wafting the sound through the brittle January air.

For all of us boys those Moguls named after Lochs seemed like vast iron horses; we believed there could be none bigger. They took freight and passenger trains alike through the mountains and along the rugged coastal section from Glasgow to the Hebrides. They used to stop for water at Crianlarich. Often there was one doing just this at dusk on a winter's evening. We used to watch the great black monster with its pilot plough encrusted with snow heralding bitter weather, as we listened, absorbed, while it struggled for breath.

We had been told by a friendly railwayman that this breathing and spluttering was a combination of the use of blower and injector, but we never thought of it like that, for to us the locomotive was not a machine at all but a living creature that had lungs which ran out of puff like the rest of us. The engine, heading North was resting and panting as an animal rests and pants regaining its strength for the long pull across the remoteness of Rannoch Moor.

The trains were said to be going to Fort William and Mallaig, and indeed the timetables confirmed this, but we boys knew better. They were going, we were sure, to the end of the rainbow, to a make-believe and wondrous land and once there, they would never stop rolling. Undoubtedly they would pause by a water-column now and again as befits a locomotive, when they would rest briefly and breathe heavily. But they never came to the terminus, for the line had no end. The tracks, we knew, crossed Inverness-shire, a county reputedly of massive distances, and then on along the road to the Isles to Heaven knows where, those splendid creatures whistling, breathing, steaming, pounding and rolling . . . rolling to the edge of the world and the end of time . . .

Later on in life some of us resolved to find out about these trains and where they went. Terence Cuneo was not only one of them, but his skills and brushwork enabled the nostalgic atmosphere and magic of steam to be captured for each and every one to enjoy and experience truly for all time.

Combermere Abbey
1982

6

Contents

The Author on the footplate of 'The Great Marquess',
the locomotive owned by Viscount Garnock.

The Railway Painting of Terence Cuneo.

The train came clanking into Balquhidder station, Scotland. A north bound express, carrying mail. I was delighted to see that she was double-headed, drawn by a couple of LMS 'Black Fives'. The lead engine was taking on water as I came up. She looked a clapped-out old girl to me. Stained with the grease of ages and showing the tell-tale burn on the bottom of the smoke box door, sure evidence of a well thrashed engine. One sand pipe hung slack and way off the driving wheel it was designed to serve. The hard voice of the blower came from both engines, sending vertical plumes of smoke into the still air and as the fireman pushed the hose clear and clanged shut the tender coalhole door, the train eased forward a length to enable the second locomotive to take on water. The lead driver climbed down and began oiling around. I flourished my footplate pass and was about to explain myself when the safety valve lifted with an earsplitting roar. The man took a cursory glance at the card and hitched a thumb at the cab. I climbed up. The fireman was baling coal into a white hot fire. He stood, legs astride, body half-turned towards the tender, then with full shovel, sent coal flying through the fire-hole in one fluid motion. To watch a fireman at work has always enthralled me. It was graceful action and looked so easy. First he threw coal up to the front of the box, then with a twist of the wrist to either side finally dropped in a load to cover the rear end fire bars. Putting down his shovel, he slammed the fire-doors together, eased the blower, opened the water feed and twisted the injector wheel. Noise in the cab subsided into the familiar gurgling rhythm of an injector which has taken satisfactorily. The fireman flicked an eye at the pressure gauge, mopped his hands on a piece of cotton waste and turning to me, winked. 'How do, mate', said he. We chatted for a moment or two. He nodded at my camera and sketch book, 'Goin' to take some pictures of our ol' engin, then? You on holiday, are you?' I explained that I was an artist working on a poster for the Railways and was here to get some mountain scenery from the footplate. 'Oh, I reckon you'll get plenty of that around here, rough ol' place, Scotland.'

The driver appeared, gave me a brief nod and set himself down in the cab seat. He was a lean hatchet-faced fellow in his late fifties and I decided, one of that breed of enginemen that didn't hold with laymen cluttering up a footplate. The fireman leant out and looked back along the train. Somewhere a whistle trilled. He turned, 'We're away, Fred,' he called and, moving over, shut off the injector and opened dampers. The driver unlatched the reversing wheel and spun the handle into full forward gear. The vacuum brake came off and as I watched, the needle in the gauge slowly rose to twenty-one inches. The driver pulled the whistle lever – two short bursts of sound – then a response from the engine behind. His hand dropped to the regulator, jerking it open. The snifting valve snapped shut. The 'Black Five' seemed to sigh and began to move, a mellow 'woomph – woomph' echoed from the engines in unison, accompanied by the intermittent hissing roar from the open cocks. We moved forward, enveloped in an opaque world of vapour. The beat of the exhaust increased. Then, in an instant, an eruption of smoke from the chimney, the footplate juddered as the driving wheels lost their grip on the rails and raced madly. The driver eased back the regulator, then again opened up. The wheels settled, bit the sand and took the load. The driver shut off the cocks and started notching back as we accelerated, leaving Balquhidder behind us in a haze of smoke.

For a quarter of a mile, the track ran straight and level, but as we swung into the first curve, the gradient ahead became apparent. Now the engines began to work. With regulators set wide and with both engines sending up a cannonade of smoke, we thundered through Glen Ogle pass. It was splendid to see and hear those steel 'shires' straining in their collars and exerting every ounce of strength they could muster, to deal with the task ahead. Clambering on to the coals I looked back at the second engine, her boiler quivering to the thrust of pistons, the voice of her exhaust thunderous beneath the pall of smoke that erupted from her chimney. I felt a surge of emotion within me. Was it pride, or perhaps delight, or was it even a sense of privilege at being able to witness this flamboyant display of might from giants of a dying era? Whatever it was, show me the diesel, or its electric counterpart, that could evoke one-tenth of the emotional romanticism these warm-hearted beasts so readily inspired.

That was but one of a wide assortment of trips I have enjoyed on footplates, both in this country and in various parts of the world. Where did it all start? Where had I contracted this strange compelling malady which was to become a constant and absorbing interest throughout my life? Who can say. But what I saw of the steam engine I worshipped, and indeed my love affair can be traced back through the dim ages of childhood.

In my mind's eye I can still see the wondrous apple-green monsters, brass domes dazzling and dimming as they flashed and faded through the sunshine of a bright day. Long copper-rimmed chimneys emitting fluffy white clouds into a child's clear blue sky. Through the eyes of a three-year-old, never was brass so bright or paint so green. The memory, too, of standing by a level-crossing, my face pressed against the wire mesh of the gate, awaiting the arrival of the train I knew must surely come. At last, the distant rumble; ground-sound swelling to thunder which shook the earth beneath sandalled feet. The snarl of steam, the shriek of a whistle and suddenly, flashing red connecting rods, rising and falling beneath a royal-blue boiler, the engine passing and immediately the rushing wind and the towering brown coaches swishing by, wheels hammering on rail-joints.

This is the little engine my father brought home when I was five years old.

Clearly a Great Eastern memory. But then, in the days proir to the amalgamation there was so much *colour* in locomotives to delight the eye of a child. The fresh warm green of the London and South Western, for instance. The maroon red of the Midland Railway. That beautiful blue of the Caledonian and the golden brown of the London Brighton and South Coast Railway. Again, I'm sure it was the *lack* of colour that put me off the London and North Western with its forbidding black engines, whereas the full bold green of the Great Western Railway locomotives with their copper rimmed chimneys and unique brass 'milk churn' safety valves, epitomised, then as now the ultimate in locomotive magnificence.

One other childhood memory can't be left out – the London Steam Bus – although it has no rightful place in our subject. These provided the greatest thrill because *real* flame came out of the bonnet! The thing to do was to get aboard quickly, scamper up the steps to the open deck and hang over the front before the bus started. As it moved away flames would often appear through the bonnet grill and one could feel the rush of hot air on one's face. These buses were delightful vehicles. They operated under the name of 'The National Bus Company' and were, I remember, painted ivory white, with elaborate gold lining and scroll work. They were almost silent and used to glide smoothly along with just the slightest hissing sound. To my mind, nothing the internal combustion engine has produced can surpass the dear old steam bus. I am happy to have known it.

I suppose I was about five years old, when one day my father brought home an exciting model steam engine. It was large and shiny and ran on a 2½″ gauge track and had with it one six-wheeled coach and a goods wagon. I shall never forget the thrill of seeing this beautiful machine puffing round and round and emitting an intoxicating aroma of hot paint, steam and methylated spirits. The fact that my father hardly allowed me to touch the engine, did little to damp my fervour, the very reverse, in fact, as from that moment on my fate was sealed and I became hopelessly hooked by the lure of steam. I was constantly drawing pictures of engines, masses of them, usually in desperate situations, such as tearing through forest fires, or being attacked by Red Indians. They were always going much too fast, with steam and smoke belching forth in riotous abundance.

It wasn't until my fifteenth Christmas that I owned my first model locomotive. This was a sturdy 2–2–0 of sheer delight with oscillating cylinders and it ran on a wooden-sleepered gauge 1 track. I had endless fun with this little tank, including singed eyebrows, constant fire hazards and a string of accidents. The seed had taken root, and as rapidly as finance would allow I began to enlarge my layout getting hold of all sorts of strange items of rolling stock. Soon I owned two more engines, both steam and both second-hand. The hazards increased, but so did my knowledge of railways. Bassett-Lowke's shop in Holborn drew me like a magnet. I developed a fine contempt for the brand new tin plate wagons sold by shops, bright in their artificial, immaculate paint work. I was quick to discover on visiting the sidings at St Ives in Cornwall, that the genuine article rarely lived up to these glossy standards and were in fact grimy, weather-beaten old things showing every sign of being the tough working vehicles that in fact, they were. Their appearance instantly appealed to me. In a very short time and with the aid of oil paint, sand, crushed coal and the like, I had my entire stock displaying a life-like ruggedness that was good to behold. Nor did the transformation stop at wagons. I set to, altering everything that was guilty of tinctorial ex-travagence. Stations, level-crossings, bridges, signals – the lot. *My* coach roofs were dirty, so were the running boards. I made faded green tarpaulins to cover the loads on some of the wagons. My tunnels and bridges were candle-smoked in just the right places. Looking back, I am certain that this quest for realism and effective accuracy in models played a decisive part in the portrayal of the Railway Scene which later I was to put on to canvas.

My interests were by no means confined to models. I would take every opportunity to get close to any engine that presented itself. I hung about stations and goods yards, explored cuttings, peered into tunnels and craned over bridges to savour the delights of smoke and steam as a train roared beneath. I occasionally managed to get myself invited up into the odd signal-box and used to make a point, when a train was standing in a station, of peering wistfully up into the engine's cab, with a convincing 'hard-done-by-under-privileged' sort of expression, which more often than not won me an invitation to come aboard. Another delight, of course was putting pennies on the line and watch a train flatten them wafer thin and to twice their size. I remember one such occasion in company with my friend, Peter Hewitt, when, surprised by the speed of the oncoming train and frantic to get our coins placed, Peter thrust on a two shilling piece (ten pence) in mistake for his penny! This financial calamity successfully cured *him* of any further love of the steam engine – two shillings in those days was a *fortune*!

At nineteen, after a somewhat perfunctory art-school training, I decided to launch myself on an unsuspecting world as an illustrator of boys' books and magazines. I was to find, only too soon, that my entry into this field hardly caused a ripple on the smooth waters of the publishing fraternity and I was hard pressed to exist. However, things

One of a series of paintings commissioned by the Rootes Group and used in calendar form.

gradually improved.

By diligence and much privation I eventually found myself a busy man, turning out a mass of pen-and-ink drawings on every conceivable subject and pocketing the princely sum of one pound sterling for each one of them!

Every once in a while a story about railways would turn up. These I tackled with relish and executed with considerable inaccuracy. My great standby, when problems arose, was *steam*. Bags of steam, introduced into my drawings in liberal doses, not only exuding from unlikely places in a locomotive's anatomy, but releasing me from the tiresome chore of having to draw wheels and valve-gear. One serial I was entrusted with for a Boy's paper called 'The Railway Wreckers' was a real horror story. In this tale, engines ploughed through crossing-gates, trains plunged into ravines. Heroes and villains struggled on footplates, and curly headed youths dropped on to carriage-tops from above. There was even the mad signalman who arranged a 'head-on' to break the monotony of his lonely vigil. Never a dull moment!

It was a year or two later that I first met Hamilton-Ellis the author and artist, when the Oxford University Press commissioned me to illustrate a number of his books. The job delighted me and I am glad to say, the finished works delighted the author, too. One particular favourite of mine was his reconstruction of the true story of an escape, during the American Civil War, in which the famous old wood-burning locomotive, 'General' played the principal part.

Ellis and I became good friends over the years, and he tells me that he purchased most of my originals from the firm and has them to this day.

In the early 1930s, my mother sold our house in St Ives and bought another in London's Bedford Park, off the Bath Road, where I had a studio on the top floor. It was whilst living here that I learnt to drive steam engines. A branch of the old West London Railway, owned by the LMS, crossed the road beside our garden. Once a day a goods train would come chugging over the crossing to shunt trucks around and into the depot on the Chiswick High Road. It didn't take long to get to know the drivers and still less time to get myself invited up on the footplate.

The first time I actually drove is an experience that will always remain in my memory. I can see myself again, up there in the cab, entranced with smells of hot oil and steam, and bathed in the warmth from the backplate and fire-box. Gazing through the cab window, fascinated by the length of boiler ahead, I gingerly reach for the regulator and at the command, jerk it smartly downwards. The engine sighs, like some monster roused from hibernation. From the chimney a mighty 'woomph-woomph' thunders out. Steam roars from the open cylinder cocks and we are *moving*! The cab quivers, the wheels squeal a protest as the boiler swings left across the points. I cannot believe that *my* puny hand has done all this; set this great metal beast rumbling obediently along its road of iron. Immediately before me the massive regulator lever, the polished brass handle of the brake valve, the heavy reversing wheel.

These instruments of control seemed unnecessarily large to one person. I was to have the privilege of knowing in later years – His Royal Highness, Prince Philip. He was sitting for an equestrian portrait which had been commissioned by the Welsh Guards, when the conversation turned to the business of driving engines as opposed to aeroplanes; 'I simply cannot understand why steam engines have to have such clumping great levers to control them', I recall him saying, 'They seem to me quite unnecessarily heavy.' His remark has given me food for thought and I am not at all sure that I gave His Royal Highness a convincing answer at the time, either! However, His observation to an extent is certainly true. Locomotive controls *are* heavy, some of them, damned heavy. I drove an engine on the Nord Railway of France once, that had a regulator stiff enough to dislocate your wrist, and a Midland tank-engine with a reversing lever that was guaranteed to slip a disc every time you touched it!

To return to a lighter theme – in the new house was my own, gauge 1 garden railway, built on trestles with nice shallow curves and a forty foot straight. We used to have enormous fun with this and sessions which invariably ended with a disaster of one sort or another. Three or four of us would run an engine each and, although we used to decide beforehand exactly how we would behave, things never seemed to work out. Either an engine ran out of fuel at a crucial moment, or it would foul the points when an express was cutting it fine in the opposite direction. A goods train would break in two in the tunnel, or fail to pull its load the required distance.

Let me introduce you to a somewhat typical session. A figure hovers over an oil-stained 'Mogul'. 'The rotten clack-valve's stuck again', he moans as he attempts to pump water against the boiler pressure. 'Well, for heaven's sake get yours off the main!' roars a voice through a hole in the garage wall. 'Mine's got about a hundred pounds of the best and I've *got* to let her go!' A safety-valve lifts somewhere. Voices shout instructions that nobody heeds. Assorted trains tear round followed by dirty-faced, wild-eyed beings who flounder along, tripping over flower beds and making wild lunges at elusive throttles.

'Look out', shrieks a voice from inside the garage, 'she's got away from me!' An engine shoots out of the hole, doing a scale speed of two hundred miles an hour! There is a concerted rush to get hold of it; somebody yelps as he grabs the hot boiler by mistake, and another catches his sleeve on the cab of his engine, which promptly falls over and bursts into flame. Help is immediately diverted to the incendiary, whereupon four sets of inflated cheeks blow the flames in all directions, improving the fire to a surprising extent. Meanwhile, the runaway leaps the track, turns a somersault in mid-air and falls like a blazing meteor into a stack of flower pots.

On one extreme occasion play was brought to a dramatic close by a deafening report followed by the sound of splintering woodwork. A boiler had burst and had shot through the next-door-neighbour's fence, ripping away three of the palings. As we stood mutely regarding the remains of a once-proud freight engine, the owner of the fence appeared from behind his battered stockade and glowered at us with acute disfavour. 'I say, Cuneo', he spluttered, his voice rising to an hysterical whinny, 'isn't this carrying things a bit *too* far?'

After my initiation on the footplate I availed myself of any opportunity to extend the experience. Of the numerous drivers on that particular 'link', one, George Bennett, became a close friend. This man, sensing my enthusiasm, took me in hand, giving me invaluable help and a sound working knowledge in handling locomotives of various classes. Some days it would be a six-coupled Midland tank that came over. On others, a big eight-coupled tender engine. Sometimes even an ancient 'Cauliflower' would come wheezing across the road but more often it was that maid-of-all-work the old London and North Western 'D' class engine. These were rough, powerful brutes but eminently practical from *my* point of view.

I became pretty efficient in the art of shunting and, believe it or not, on more than one occasion, was allowed to operate alone on the footplate whilst George and his fireman lapped tea in the signal box. All very casual and homely, but that's how things were on our good old Bath Road line! One day whilst I was driving and looking back over the tender I saw the shunter give me the 'rapid back

One of a series of paintings done for the firm Newton Chambers – Sheffield. This was the actual engine which was personally presented to me by the firm.

up' signal. The engine was running 'light' at the time and the track wound in a sharp 'S' out of my line of vision. In other words, I could not see the entire road between me and the coal trucks in the far distance. Had we been behaving correctly, the fireman would have glanced out from his side to make certain the road was clear. In actual fact, he and the driver were warming their backsides by the fire-door, discussing the pruning of raspberry canes. Winding the reversing wheel, I gave the regulator a sharp jerk and with a mighty bark from the stack we were off. The tender wheels squealed as we struck the curve and the exhaust pounded great guns. Suddenly – 'Shut 'er off!' yelled the fireman. The driver's hand closed over mine as we thrust the regulator up and then, a throaty hiss as the vacuum brake was flung over. 'Blimey', breathed the driver, 'there's a brake van on the road!'

The engine was slowing down but we had gained considerable way. All at once I saw the forgotten van, slap ahead – there was an all mighty crash that nearly knocked us off our feet. How that wagon stayed on the road is a miracle. In horror I seemed to see it leap into the air, dust flying from every pore. Then it set off at a horrid pace towards the waiting trucks. The next moment can only be described as electric. The fireman shouted advice to the startled shunters, the shunters jostled one another, then tore off down the line in pursuit. Shunters' poles seemed to flay the air; windows were flung up and heads appeared, looking up and down the line. The suspense was appalling. I could not take my eyes from that rolling brake-van. Seconds ticked by – and the gap closed. The decent quiet of the morning was suddenly shattered. An unholy clashing and clanging of scores of outraged buffers broke like a fiends' orchestra upon the neighbourhood. Then – a dreadful hush. Craning from the motionless engine, I saw the brake van rocking gently, one window shattered, amidst a rising pall of coal and brick dust.

It was still on the metals!

Although unaware of it at the time, the practical, if somewhat unorthodox, experience gained on that little branch line proved of inestimable value to me in my subsequent approach to the portrayal of locomotives on canvas. When one actually drives an engine and gets the 'feel' of it, one becomes overwhelmingly conscious of its power and even more important, of its *weight*. This then, is the predominating factor. Thus, to make paintings of locomotives convincing, one must be able to *paint* this illusion of weight in much the same way as an artist, specialising in birds, must be able to paint an illusion of weightlessness. I have seen so many works where the ability to achieve either quality is totally lacking. Those train paintings, that give the impression that one good sneeze is enough to blow them off the track, or conversely bird pictures in which one is dismally conscious of leaden forms, struggling like over-loaded bombers trying to get themselves off the tarmac. Don't ask me how these illusions are achieved in paint; I only know that somehow it can be done. Perhaps it comes from an unconscious sympathy and true understanding of one's subject.

France, 1940
Illustrated London News.

Study for Poster, 'Giants Refreshed'.

At this stage in my career my work began transporting me into wider and more varied fields and railway paintings enjoyed but a meagre place in this broadening spectrum. I was now illustrating widely and quite apart from boys stuff I was beginning to get recognition from the majority of the countries leading magazines and periodicles, such as, *The Illustrated London News, Nashe's, The Strand, Good Housekeeping* and the *Wide World Magazine*. This latter monthly through its diversity of story matter, gave me the facility to tackle a truly enormous variety of subjects, which experience has stood me in good stead throughout my painting life. I learnt to work fast, too, as press dates *had* to be kept, however busy one was. It was a great schooling, but a hard grind.

As war loomed nearer, many of these journals folded up, but curiously, I never felt the jolt, as war magazines appeared to fill the gap. Even during the early part of my army life I was still able to turn out the odd press illustration for the *ILN*, *The War* and *War Illustrated*.

It was not until 1948 that an odd event brought me once more back into the realm of steam. During a leave from the army in '42 I had sketched a lovely old Essex water-mill, and soon after the picture had been exhibited at the London Sketch Club annual exhibition, I received a letter from the PRO of the London and North Eastern Railway, asking me to call. He told me that he had seen the painting and would like to use it as a 'Double Royal' (upright) poster and would like me to make a copy of the work to fit the necessary proportion. Shortly after this poster appeared on the hoardings he again contacted me.

This time, to go up to Doncaster and make studies for a 'Quad-Royal' poster of one of their A4 Pacifics, which was being painted. This was truly one of the moments of my life and up I went with alacrity! That same afternoon I was led, wide-eyed, into a huge and clean locomotive paint-shop. There before me towered the magnificent Gresley Pacific, her body gleaming in fresh blue livery, whilst beside her and slightly in front stood an equally elegant A3 in contrasting LNER green. God, what a picture it made and the whole scene was enhanced by the delightfully incongrous presence in the foreground, of an elderly employee, *hand* painting fire extinguishers and numerals on the white face of a pressure gauge! A made to measure composition if *ever* I saw one. There was even a shop cat, sitting there beside a bogie, in grave contemplation. Incredible! That cat, incidently, was a character and as cunning as the proverbial barrel of monkeys. It seemed always 'in an interesting condition', producing innumerable kittens, but try as they might, the men could *never* discover where she kept her families. It was only when the foreman one day, gave orders for an old tank engine to be moved to make way for another paint job, that 'Sissie' was seen to jump up on the engine's buffer-beam and enter the slightly open smoke-box door. Presently, she reappeared, carrying a marmalade kitten in her mouth. That poster, 'Giants Refreshed', proved a turning point and was the reason that I was entrusted with producing an entire set of British Railway Prestige Posters.

What a thrilling commission it was, full of both interest and excitement and not without the added spice of danger and the occasional hair-raising situation. Almost every subject had its moments. The Royal Albert Bridge for instance. As a child coming up from Cornwall to school at Sutton Valence, I would hang from the window and watch the great tubes of Brunel's masterpiece float past my head. Little did I know then, that one day I would be asked to make a poster commemorating the centenary of his bridge.

How many people, I wonder, have had an express train specially stopped for them? I went up on the footplate of a London train at Plymouth, with authority to stop the locomotive anywhere I chose in the vicinity of Saltash Bridge – for exactly *thirty seconds*, no more. As we approached I gave the word and we came to a halt sixty yards from the archway. I climbed up on the coals and began rapidly sketching. Just before the time was up I glanced back along the train. There were faces at almost every window! I could see astonishment in some of them and could imagine their reaction. 'Why have we stopped here and what on earth is that fat head doing standing on the tender?'

The viewpoint, however did not prove practical, and before deciding the final position, I walked the bridge at dawn, throughout the day and even during the night. Apart from making notes I had to keep a wary look out for locomotives, which could creep up on one as quiet as cats and from both directions on that speed restricted single track.

I finally decided upon a position on the Cornish side which enabled me to use the curve in the track as a foil and thus show both front and side of the bridge and the water beneath. The only way this could be achieved was to maroon myself on the top of one of the stone columns, which stood a good two feet out from the bridge itself! From this airy perch I made a working drawing of the scene. When the job was completed I was booked by BR to go home on the London train. I entered a first class compartment complete with suitcase but covered in dirt and grease, intending to change on the train. The sole occupant of the compartment was a dignified old lady sitting in a corner seat. She gave me a startled glance. 'Do please excuse my appearance', I reassured her, 'But I've been painting Saltash Bridge'. The old lady's face lit in a sudden smile. 'Oh how *nice*', she said, 'I do hope you chose a pretty colour.'

I wonder if the traveller, looking at a poster on the station wall, as he stands awaiting his train, ever stops to think: 'How did the fellow manage to get that incredible effect?', or 'That lighting is remarkable, you feel the whole thing is *alive*!', Or 'Good heavens, just look at the way he's dealt with that solid foreground, it absolutely *makes* the picture!' Very seldom, I fear. Usual reactions are far more basic. The person either likes the thing or he doesn't. If he does, he will study it, for its technical attributes, or for the pleasure its subject matter affords him. If he doesn't he will drift off and goggle at the girl in a soap advertisement or something, next door. Nevertheless, you have presented him with a 'fait accompli' to evaluate as he sees fit and he quite rightly, remains oblivious of the hazards and thought searchings that have gone into the making of

Working on the drawing of the Royal Albert Bridge – Saltash.

14

the painting. Afterall, why *should* he concern himself with your problems? He didn't *ask* you to paint the wretched thing! He merely observes what is there, on the wall in front of him.

Be this as it may, you might be surprised to hear that a great number of people really *do* want to know just how, 'that particular effect was obtained.' Or, '– how that solid foreground made the picture'. In other words, their liking for a work stimulates a desire to know more about its background. Stories or even an adventure that might lie behind its conception are enthusiastically received. I get asked innumerable questions on these points. 'Was that one done on the spot?' 'There *must* be a story behind this, isn't there? Do tell us'. And so on.

I can give a firm nod to both the above questions. Every one of my B.R. posters was done on the spot and every one of them has a story. So, in the hope that the majority of my readers are those who ask just such questions, I feel it is worth recounting a few experiences of poster work and other railway commissions.

How the memories come flooding back as I write! Memories that are precious, with experiences that I would not have exchanged for any part of my working life. Riding through an African night on one of the big Rhodesian 'Garratts', listening to the roar of water cascading over the Victoria Falls as our engine rolls across the high trestles that span the Zambezi. Watching the beam from the head-lamp pierce the dark mystery of the Wanki game reserve as we steam slowly on our way down to Bulawayo. These fine engines, incidently, were, to my

knowledge, the only ones that ever carried three men on the foot-plate; a Rhodesian driver and fireman and an African, whose job it was to trim coal down from the back of the tender. At the time I was on an assignment which necessitated extensive travel throughout South Africa and Rhodesia, painting a set of canvases covering almost every activity of The Anglo American Corporation. This not only brought me into contact with trains but took me through a vast network of gold, diamond and copper mines and into situations as hairy as any I have enjoyed in railway involvement. To quote but two. The first, a 'shaft sinking' scene in the Orange Free State, which entailed being dropped 4,400 feet down a raw shaft, at 45 miles an hour in an open bucket. The second, being tied to a tree on a life-line (presumably for my own protection!) at the edge of a one thousand foot drop, to paint the famous diamond 'pipe' at the Premier mine, Pretoria. When my Zulu police boy actually saw them fixing a rope round my waist and tying the other end to a tree, he rolled on his back, kicked his legs in the air and nearly had hysterics.

Then again, riding a locomotive through the Canadian Rockies on a perfect November morning, with the sun bright, the air crystal clear and two inches of snow between the metals. As we roll down the Great Divide towards Kicking Horse Pass the engineer calls me across the cab. He points a gloved hand to where the portals of the famous spiral tunnel stand, one above the other and way below us. I see a toy-like string of box-cars and a caboose slowly entering the lower portal, whilst immediately above it, three locomotives emerge dragging

Study for "Royal Albert Bridge, Saltash Poster".

the train upwards. What a sight, but how different from the experience in Ethiopia of driving an old Italian 'Mallet' up the cork-screw road from the Red Sea port of Massawa to the heights of Asmara. This incredibly engineered 2 foot gauge climbs seven thousand feet in under forty miles and plunges into something like forty-five tunnels on the way. One comes storming out of one of these, with all but the grate-bars going up through the smoke-stack, braces oneself as the engine jerks for a swinging curve and gazes down at a terrifying precipice on one side and ragged crags rearing up on the other. Then, almost before one can gulp in a lung full of pure air, the engine's entered yet another tunnel, exhaust pounding the ears and sulphurous smoke assailing the nostrils. And so on and so on, tunnel after tunnel. Nevertheless, it was not a trip to be missed. When I finally arrived at the hotel, covered with coal dust, the hall porter did all in his power to remove me from the premises.

There was a ridiculous affair, too, in India. By way of explanation I should say at this point, that as well as steam engines I do spend a lot of my time galloping around the world doing my best to complete commissions often requested by the Army. My attempts to recreate on canvas the famous battle scenes of various Regiments started thirty years ago and since then I have completed quite a number of large Ceremonial canvases as well. These have added a further delightful diversion with paintings necessitating portraits of various members of our Royal family. But I digress. I had finished a series of battle scenes in the Malayan jungle for the Royal Green Jackets and the 10th Gurkhas and came up into India under the wing of the latter where I stayed as a guest at Barrackpore Transit Camp. The adjutant detailed to meet me at Dum Dum Airport was a keen amateur artist and in no time we were out together in an Army Land Rover sketching all and sundry. One day we came across a locomotive taking on water outside Barrackpore station. On an impulse I said to the Adjutant, who spoke excellent Bengali, 'Tell the crew I'm a well known engine driver from England and would

like to drive their locomotive'. This colourful message was duly shouted up to the cab, whereupon, to our mutual astonishment, the Sikh driver invited us both to climb aboard. The driver's seat and its arm-rest were vigorously wiped clear of grime and I was invited 'when the light changes – to proceed, please'.

The crossing gates closed, a signal winked green. I pulled open the throttle and as the locomotive began to move toward the station, the fireman held down the whistle-chain sending such a belching cloud of steam across the boiler that it was impossible to see anything in the form of pedestrians, dogs, carts or chickens that still might lie in the path of our 'cow-catcher'. Five hundred yards beyond the station I drew the train to a halt. We warmly thanked the driver and climbed down. The following day we repeated the exercise, with, believe it or not, *identical* results! This time I was able to drive the entire way to the next station as we had taken the precaution of sending the Gurkha with the Land Rover ahead, to await our arrival. Surprising what a bit of audacity will achieve!

Many will remember, in 1970, a disastrous fire that virtually destroyed the grand old Britannia Bridge that spans the Menai Straits, in Wales. Shortly after this sad event, the late Sir Richard Summers of Shotton Steel Works, for whom I had painted a number of canvases of the company's blast-furnaces and rolling-mills, rang me in a state of great distress, imploring me to come up and paint him a picture of his dearly loved bridge before it was demolished.

Two days later I was on the site and we both walked through the burnt out 'tubes' of Robert Stephenson's engineering tour de force. It was a depressing experience. Inside, the rails sagged like telegraph wires. The wrought iron 'boxes' were distorted and, in places, fractured from top to bottom and everywhere there prevailed the deadly aftermath stench of fire. We walked out into the sunshine. Ahead of us, on either side of the tracks, magnificent but indifferent to the tragedy behind them, squatted two of

This locomotive heading 'The Canadian', was one of the diesels I rode on through the Rockies, from Calgary, down through The Great Divide and into British Columbia.

Driving an old Baldwin 'mogul', in Ontario, Canada.

One of the powerful little 'Mallet' tank engines pounding its way up from the Red Sea port to Massawa, Ethiopia.

the gargantuan, Egyptian lions which have guarded both ends of the bridge since its conception. I strolled along the line ahead of these beasts and from the curve on the up-line, looked back at the scene. The composition was perfect. I knew I had found the spot from which to make a drawing. The lions supplied a strong foreground interest and beyond them the whole length of the bridge showed in telling perspective with the water of the Straits in view beneath. The completed canvas, however, showed no signs of devastation, as it was Sir Richard's express wish to own a picture showing the Bridge in all its Victorian splendour. It was at his suggestion, too, that I painted in the locomotive of the Irish Mail, steaming majestically out into the sunlight on the up-road.

Another great bridge recalls somewhat different emotions. In all, I have painted three different scenes of the Forth Bridge, the last, depicting the 'Flying Scotsman' steaming beneath the girders from the north. This was back in the days of Alan Pegler who once owned the engine and was, in fact, the first time the locomotive had ever crossed the Firth. The commission was both amusing and exhilarating. I boarded the engine (which I have been allowed to drive on occasions) at Edinburgh and the four of us, Alan, the driver, the fireman and myself rode her down to the bridge, pulling behind us a single coach containing a number of Alan's friends and assorted goodies of a nutritious and thirst quenching nature.

The form was to drive along the bridge until I felt that we had reached a possible view point. Then, the train would be stopped. I would leap out, run forward and assess the resulting composition. This was the pattern and it went on for quite some time, with me hanging from the cab steps, leaping along the track, shouting to the driver and generally working myself into a state of breathless dedication. Frequently things were rudely interrupted, through the event of another train being signalled, whereupon we would have to reverse briskly back into a siding to allow the wretched thing to pass; then back on to

the bridge once more. When, at last, I found the spot I wanted and sat by the trackside sketching away, it became increasingly exasperating to see the 'Scotsman' suddenly set off backwards, time after time and disappear from sight. However, this is one of the accepted joys of open air work! Eventually the sketch was finished and I was able to retire gratefully to the warmth of the footplate, and on through the corridor in the tender to the coach, where a well earned drink awaited me.

My *first* visit to the Forth Bridge holds equally vivid memories. A bitter morning in February and the day on which King George VI died. I heard the sad news as I was climbing the rigging to the catwalks, 25 feet above rail level, and 175 feet over the waters of the Firth. Working conditions here were frankly terrifying. Although swaddled in flying suit, duffel coat, balaclava and mittens to say nothing of long woollen underwear (a legacy from my Army days), I was frozen. The screaming of the wind through the girders was so intense that trains, usually noisy on the bridge, passed beneath me in ghostly silence, their smoke snatched by the gale. It was then decided, since my position seemed insecure, to send men up with sheets of canvas, which they proceeded to lash to the hand-rails in an effort to protect me from the worst of the wind. However, these billowed into me with such vigour that I was nearly thrust backwards off the cat-walk and they had to be rapidly dismantled. Now my fingers became so numb that I could hardly hold a pencil. When finally the drawing was finished and I was ready to go down, a feeling of near panic took hold of me. One look down at that dark, surging water miles below, that appeared to race through the myriad lattice of the girders, had me in a sweat. Fixing my sketch-book on a string around my neck, I crawled on all fours along the cat-walk, descending the ladder down to the great tubes with eyes tight shut, hoping nobody was around to witness my discomfort. When I did finally get to the bottom, I was shown the wind chart. I had been sketching in a 53 mile

On the footplate of the 'Flying Scotsman'.

Making studies for the poster 'The Forth Bridge'.

an hour gale!

'Track Laying by Night' for the Southern was perhaps the most chaotic of the set of poster commissions. On the night chosen, track was being laid through Wandsworth Common station and it was pouring! The scene was a floodlit hive of activity. The track-laying train would come in, lower a forty foot length on to the bed of the other 'road', then set off down the line to deposit its next forty footer and so on. Immediately the track was down, gangs of men would close in and tamp down the ballast, bolt on the fish plates and hurry along to the next length. And had *I* to hurry! Scribbling lightning notes of the scene as a whole (no camera) and as many action sketches as I could manage in the time. The fact that I ran my finger on to a razor blade (kept in my pocket to sharpen pencils) did nothing to simplify matters. My drawing was now not only wet but smeared with blood into the bargain and what with leaping along forty-foot spans of slippery sleepers, clutching a Tilley flood lamp in one hand and a sketch book in the other and being barged by the work crew, it was hardly surprising that I left the Common at four o'clock that morning, exhausted. Yet I enjoyed every sodden, blood-soaked moment of it.

Who was it who said to me: 'It must be lovely sitting there in your cozy studio painting all those super pictures.' That fellow should have worked for the railways!

The footplate scene, 'Clear Road Ahead', for instance. This started quietly enough at Old Oak Common shed, where the fireman of a 'Castle' had to dig a hole for me in the coals, so that I sat comfortably in the tender, at the correct height to make a detailed drawing of the boiler backplate. Next, a trip to Reading, perched in the tender of 'Monmouth Castle' heading an express to the west country. This was *not* so comfortable! With one leg braced against the hand-brake I attempted a series of action sketches of driver and fireman, with old 'Monmouth' hitting it up at seventy miles an hour. You should try it! Cinders, coal-dust and wind flung themselves at me, the sketch-book juddered in my hand and at least two pages ripped from the pad and took off in free flight over Berkshire. The driver was useless for my purpose. He stood there, about as dynamic as a wax policeman! But his fireman was great and I gathered some splendid action details from him. At Reading I left the west bound, tore across the bridge in time to catch another train, drawn by a 'Hall' class just pulling out, Paddington bound. That, too, was a ride to remember. This particular 'Hall' had a reputation for being a 'roller'. We roared through Slough with the front end behaving like the bows of a tramp steamer in a gale! How the old girl stayed on the road I shall never know but I was busy and hadn't time to be scared. This driver was exactly what I wanted. There he was, hand resting lightly on the vacuum brake, body a graceful line, one foot on his grub-box, his backside braced against the cabside. I worked like mad, scratching and scrawling as we plunged along. The train had been 15 minutes late at Reading but we came clanking into Paddington bang on time.

I feel pretty sure that the average person watching the sleek express steaming by, imagines that her cab affords almost as smooth a ride as do the coaches that flow behind her. I hate to shatter this illusion, but with few exceptions, steam locomotives are rugged brutes, which, apart from emitting the accepted sounds of escaping steam and pulsing exhaust, jerk and roll and orchestrate these girations with metalic clashes, squeaks and rumbles. Personally, I love this pot-pouri of movement and sound and find one gets quickly used to standing square on a deck without being constantly jerked off balance.

The worst ride I ever had was on an old 'Black 5' in the Highlands. On this engine, every time the driving wheels came round there was a clashing jar on the footplate like a blow from Thor's Hammer! I crossed over to the driver. 'What's wrong?' I yelled in his ear, 'Is she falling apart?' The man turned and gave me a laconic stare. 'Bearings', he shouted back. 'But this is a good engine, mister. You want to ride one of the *real* bad 'uns. Know what we do when we get a bad 'un?' I shook my head. 'We take out our teeth and put 'em in our pocket, before the engine bloody well knocks 'em out of our heads, for us!'

As mentioned earlier, this earthy, practical participation is, in my opinion, essential for establishing authenticity which somehow *must* be injected into paintings of this sort. It is only physical involvement, this 'living the part', finding out what makes it all tick, that can make a finished work ring true, even in the eyes of those who have no technical appreciation of its merits.

However, there comes a time when a halt must be called. When escape from this total involvement becomes imperative.

At such times, I drop *everything*, get out a paint-box and camp-stool and go in search of the quietest landscape I can lay eyes on. I paint trees, boat and river scenes. I get myself abroad – paint Arabs in Marrakesh, still-life, flowers, a portrait of my granddaughter – *anything* that spells relaxation and tranquility. When not in the mood for painting at all I saddle up my horse 'Shadow', and go riding over the Surrey heaths. Believe me, there are no finer recipes for keeping one's working outlook both fresh and vigorous.

A poster I particularly enjoyed painting was of a signal-box, entitled, 'On Early Shift'. This showed the interior of a busy one-man box on the LNER main line, near Barnet just south of Greenwood tunnel, now alas, dismantled. I attended all the shifts, the early, the midday and the night, in order to decide which would shape best, pictorially. Although I finally chose the early one, I well remember the splendid character on the night shift. He was a signalman of the old school who took a terrific pride in his job and in the appearance of the box itself. He would never dream, for instance, of touching the levers without a chamois leather between his hands and the steel. One night I had taken several friends down to see the box at work and the old man delighted us with stories of his early days on the railway. My wife asked how he managed to sleep during the day. 'Well, you see', he answered, 'Its

Making studies on board 'The Great Marquess'.

all right until them young fellers start running their motorbikes up and down me back passage.'

I had another much less comfortable experience during my time at Greenwood. A 'light' engine had been placed on a nearby siding to enable me to establish proportions for the A4 pacific featured in the picture. When finished with the engine moved off and as she came past I swung up into the cab and rode down the line and into the tunnel. I did this on impulse as I needed reference for a locomotive entering a tunnel for another painting I was involved with and this seemed an ideal opportunity. At the far end the driver stopped to let me down and I set off to walk back through the bore. The tunnel was under half-a-mile long and straight, so that I could see daylight at either end. Before I was half way, I became aware of a tiny plume of smoke coming from the direction of London. A fast train, running north. I turned and scrutinised the track behind me. Confident that nothing could catch me in the back, I planted myself between the rails of the up-line and prepared to enjoy a new sensation. The north-bound approached rapidly; I could see the swaying boiler front getting bigger and bigger until suddenly, it had entered the portals and came roaring towards me, a monstrous silhouette in the surrounding gloom. I was deafened by the thunder of exhaust and the clash of side rods. The proportions of the engine appeared grotesque. Now it was abreast and tearing past. I swung on my heel to watch its progress and as I did so a blanket seemed to envelope me. I could see nothing! I brought my hands up to my face. *They weren't there*! Only a solid darkness that pressed against my eyes. I wonder whether you can appreciate this sensation? One moment I had been watching a train, the next, because of the smoke, I was plunged into a world of utter blackness. With the roar of the passing coaches ringing in my ears, I turned once more towards London – but everything had gone; the darkness was complete. Then, I became aware of another sound. A steady rhythmic pulsing. Listening, I felt the hair prickle on my scalp! A whistle wailed somewhere and the pulsing seemed to grow and be coming from everywhere at once. Now the tunnel began to vibrate about me and I could make out the steady 'rhum-rhum-rhum' of a moving locomotive. The whistle sounded again. Nearer! 'If you want to live and paint again, you'd better get moving' my fairy godmother whispered, 'You're standing on the up-line, remember!'

An ice-like hand seemed to grip me as I realised I hadn't a clue which way to move. In turning I had lost all sense of direction. But move I must. The coaches had gone and now the tunnel reverberated horribly to the oncoming train and a sudden draught buffeted my face. Noise was all around – everywhere; the very nearness of it seemed to numb my senses. I took a step in the darkness, then another. My toe struck something hard and I all but fell. One of the metals. Fine, but *which one*? I took a chance and with arm outstretched, stepped over the rail. Almost at once my hands came in contact with the wall. Thank God!

I still wasn't in the clear. The wall had been far too

First rough composition for the poster 'Track Laying By Night'.

Making a detail drawing of the interior of Greenwood signal box for the poster 'On Early Shift'.

close to the metals, which meant I was not opposite an embrasure and stood a chance of being caught between engine and tunnel. As in a nightmare, I floundered, feeling blindly along the wall. I saw a lurid glow racing towards me. Breaking into a run I stumbled forward. All at once my hands clutched at space and I knew I had found an alcove. Flattening myself against the narrow recess I looked back – the engine came on me, a towering black shape. I felt the hot breath from her cylinder and water splashing from the injector overflow pipe. I leant against the wall, panting. With each wagon that clattered past, more light filtered back into the tunnel as the engine sucked along the bore, the smoke from the previous train. Finally, the brake-van came rattling past and I stepped from my 'hide' and started to walk towards the tunnel mouth. As I left the archway behind me, the hot sunshine and the good fresh air seemed a gift from heaven. I glanced at my hands and at my clothes, and shuddered.

Rather less disturbing to the emotions, if a shade discomforting to the 'inner man', were the circumstances of the initial study for the poster, 'Port to Port'.

This shows the bridge of the British Railway's Steam Ship, 'Invicta', with helmsman at the wheel and her captain gazing out towards a sunlit French coast. Just the tonic, in fact, to reassure the most sceptical traveller that a 'life on the ocean wave' is nothing if not beneficial to health and happiness.

The Invicta was a splendid old cross-channel steamer, with a fine war record and an efficient pair of stabilisers. My wife and I had made many a trip in her on the Dover – Calais run, but this time I was here to work. We arrived on the Boat Train on a bright and breezy morning. I felt fighting fit and as hungry as a hunter. As soon as we came aboard we made straight for the dining saloon to be assured of an early lunch, as I was anxious to be on the bridge and start my drawing soon after leaving harbour.

The fact that the ship spent her time bumping against the fender-posts even whilst in harbour, should perhaps have made me question the wisdom of choosing trifle as a sweet. However . . .!

The siren bellowed its farewell, then bellowed again. The gangway was pulled clear, bells rang and, we were away, heading smoothly for the harbour mouth. I escorted my wife to our cabin (courtesy of British Railways), collected my gear and went up on the bridge. Captain Waters, whom I knew, welcomed me with outstretched hand, showed me around, describing various technical impedimenta. I then moved about on my own searching for the view point I wanted. By the time I had found it and was ready to work, we were out into the Channel and things had begun to alter. There were 'white horses' everywhere, a stiff wind seemed to have sprung from nowhere and the ship had begun to pitch. I worked, concentrating like mad and getting the whole thing 'laid in'; the action of the helmsman, shape of the binnacle housing and the positioning of the ship's telegraph on the right. What I earnestly tried *not* to do, was to look at the way in which the bows dipped, crashing into the sea, disappearing with a shudder into a wall of water, which then came lashing against the bridge windows. In retrospect, I am convinced that the action of sketching, with ones head moving constantly up and down, up and down, from subject to sketch-book was partly responsible for a strange feeling which began to creep over me. I had an overwhelming desire to swallow and was aware of a cold sweat gathering around my forehead. The captain was chatting amusingly, recounting various nautical anecdotes, but I found, as the minutes went by, a marked disinclination to listen to stories and in particular those embracing a maritime flavour! Suddenly – I realised! Now, even fearful to swallow, I shut my sketch-book and turned to the Captain.

'I've got all I want, now, thanks', I croaked, treating the surprised man to a leering grimace, which I hoped would pass for a care-free smile and made a dive for the door. Skidding down the ladder in a thoroughly unsea-man-like manner, I staggered into the cabin. 'Give me an Alka-seltzer', I gasped, 'For God's sake!' My wife took one look at the sallow green face before her. 'Alka-seltzer won't help you, chum – you're *sea sick*!'

How discerning women are, and so often unfuriatingly right! However, the following week I returned to Dover, where the whole scene was reconstructed, with Waters and his helmsman adopting the necessary poses to suit my purpose. But this time, the S.S. Invicta was securely moored and motionless, in Dover harbour! Give me locomotives – every time!

There's a postscript to this harrowing tale. When the work had been duly delivered, I received a request from British Railways. 'Could I possibly paint a blue-striped jersey on my mouse so that people would *know* that he was intended as a joke? Otherwise they might think our ships are rat infested!'

By the way, if any of you should be 'Mouse hunters', I must point out, that the Mouse only came into being towards the end of 1953 and therefore one or two of the illustrations in this book could be of pre-Mouse period!

Before recounting perhaps, one final story of these, 'on site' ambulations, I should like you to appreciate, that, important as such sessions are, they constitute but a scaffolding for what will eventually appear as a highly finished painting in oils. Of course, it goes without saying that these so called scaffolding-sketches, action scribbles, drawings, photographic references, colour-notes and verbal information etc., are of signal importance, as without them the final work could never materialise.

The next stage is different. The initial excitement is over and back in the studio I face a large rectangle of virgin canvas that is waiting for paint. A pencil sketch is a spontaneous visual expression, but a full-blooded painting has to be constructed and carefully composed and the problems this can present, believe me, are legion. In the first place a good composition must be devised from the bits and pieces that have been brought back, including a sound colour balance. An artist must concentrate effects of light and shade, playing one against the other and thus being able to build a design that will compel attention toward the significant passages in the painting he intends to bring forward.

This does not always come easily and often alterations have to be made time after time before the desired effect is achieved. I have wiped out parts of a painting five or even six times before being satisfied with what I am trying to convey. This is worrying and infuriating, but it has to be faced and these are times when one just longs to kick something – or somebody. But struggle on I must, occasionally despairing that I will ever master such an infernal mess. There are no short cuts, no useful 'cover ups'. Those blissful days, when slapping on clouds of steam to hide the tricky parts was the perogative of the hack illustrator, no longer exist. In the sphere of railway portraiture I face the most ruthless critics of all time. These people demand that their engines look like engines and rightly so. But I assure you there are few things more arduous to portray, than boiler elipses, spoked driving-wheels and convincing looking valve-gear! In spite of such pressures *I* remain my severest critic and as you will have realised, am prepared to go to considerable lengths to satisfy my inner convictions that things are *right*. I find, too, that I wage a ceaseless struggle between satisfying the engineer on one hand and retaining my integrity and individuality as a painter of something that isn't just a 'run of the mill' piece of commercialism on the other.

An example will perhaps make this clearer. Many years ago I was commissioned by the firm of Massey Harris to paint a series, showing each of their agricultural appliances operating under natural farming conditions. Tractors, combine-harvesters, muck-spreaders, seed-drills etc., and of course, I was given access to the machines themselves to work from, all complete in their shining Massey Harris red and buff-yellow paint.

When my first painting went in, the firm was shocked beyond belief to see their proud red tractor portrayed in grubby faded paint, with a dent in the fuel tank and evidence of rust and mud everywhere. However, after the weeping and wailing had died down, I pointed out that to dirty the tractor did nothing to diminish its status, but did a very great deal to accentuate the conviction that a Massey Harris product was capable of standing up to gruelling hard work under any conditions. The resulting

First compositional rough for the poster 'Port to Port', made after my marine experience!

argument was long and at times heated, but I won and in all subsequent illustrations was given a free hand to 'rough up' their equipment to my heart's content, in much the same way as, in my youth I had 'roughed up' my own miniature railway wagons.

I believed in what I did then and I have believed in this approach ever since. A piece of working machinery can never, under any circumstances resemble the show-room model.

The habit I have developed, too, of a rigid self criticism, I regard as one of the most rewarding aspects of my career. For instance, every evening when I take a bath before dinner, the current painting I am working on goes into the bathroom with me! I prop the canvas against the wall, recline back in nice, warm water with a vodka-and-tonic in the soap-dish and a toe on the hot tap and scrutinise my work, mercilessly laying bare the very roots of what I am trying to express. Here, in the steamy detachment of a bathroom I make crucial decisions. 'That piece on the left wants softening', or 'The shadow in the foreground is much too blue, it wants warming up', or 'I havn't drawn the taper on the boiler of the "King" correctly, it's a bit too steep', and so on.

The following morning sees me acting on each one of these conclusions and in almost every case, with bene-ficial results. But then, every subject is different and each presents its own problems. Painting doesn't always come as easily to me, as many people seem to imagine. It can be a damnably difficult, maddening and frustrating profession, but of course, the most completely absorbing and enchanting occupation this world could offer.

If the encounter in Greenwood tunnel can be regarded as one of my more alarming associations with Railways, I am not sure that my latest effort depicting the new Advanced Passenger Train leaving Euston at night, should not qualify as the most dangerous.

It was Sir Peter Parker who asked me to undertake the commission, to be used primarily as a finale in a calendar of twelve railway paintings. I cannot remember, now, whose idea it was to show the new electric flyer heading out into the night, whilst behind, in ghostly array, the steam giants of yesterday wait at the platform heads, but anyway, that was to be the theme for 'Into the Eighties'.

Arrangements were duly made, with the result that I spent a warm and peaceful day sitting on a box beside the line, making a detailed working drawing of the APT as she stood empty on a siding. I also took the opportunity to explore the train. I was immensely impressed.

The next stage was to get the Euston side of things going and thus arrangements were put in hand to enable me to work on the tracks during the night. The chosen evening was fine and still. At the platform end, I was introduced to my 'protectors'; and given a bright orange waistcoat to wear over my jacket. Having tied myself into this colourful garb, the three of us set off down the platform slope and on to the tracks.

You must remember, I had already made my drawing of the APT, so now the problem was to choose a position amongst a bewildering network of rails, which would not only enable me to paint the APT in the identical perspective to that of my drawing, but which would afford a clear view of at least six platform-heads from which to show my dear old steam locomotives. The task was made no easier by the fact that the APT was not available to pose, so there was no alternative other than to observe train after train coming out from the station and catch one, in the *split second* that it occupied the position I wanted. No easy task, I assure you, as, before I could feel fully satisfied with any one of the trains, I needed to move freely from track to track, trying every possible sequence of position. It was here that the nightmare started.

Things were not too bad while there was still sufficient light to see which way points were thrown, but, as night closed in this became impossible and one was in constant danger of getting run down! Trains came in and out in a never ending flow, rumbling past at 10 to 15 miles an hour and although sometimes their lights appeared to be almost in profile to where we stood, they would often change direction and come straight towards us, on the very track in the centre of which I stood!

It was pretty hair-raising and after nearly an hour, with my two 'look-out' men constantly interrupting concentration by grabbing me by the arm and moving me from the path of an oncoming train, the tension began to tell. Hardly surprising, as there was hardly any time to make a careful and calculated step, across metals, electric junction-boxes, dwarf-signals and the like and, indeed, almost none at all if one should trip whilst doing so! But, at last the job was done. I closed the sketch-book and turned to my guardians. 'I guess that's about it', I said, 'Lets go home'. Never have I seen expressions of such utter relief on men's faces. 'Thank God that's over', said one of them, 'We've never enjoyed anything less!'

Perhaps unwittingly I have struck a prophetic note in drawing this medley of experience to a close with a vignette account of the Advanced Passenger Train. For today assuredly, is the era of electric power, of streamlined locomotives and smoother, cleaner and ever faster rail transport.

All this I know and appreciate. The world demands that we progress and that old methods must of necessity be superseded by the hand of enterprise and invention.

The steam locomotive has been superseded and nothing can ever bring it back as a means of general transportation. But I thank God that, as an artist, I was in time to witness the last great days of this fascinating, warm-hearted monster, that for well over a century has cast it witchery over countless millions.

Never again the haunting note of a whistle
Nor the ring of a fireman's shovel on the rim of a fire-box
Never again the hiss of steam or the pulsing thunder of a working locomotive.
Never again. But for those of us who heard such sounds, memory of them will forever remain.

THE END

 ESSEX

TRAVEL BY RAIL

1859 *Centenary* 1859
ROYAL ALBERT BRIDGE SALTASH
WESTERN REGION   DESIGNED AND BUILT BY ISAMBARD KINGDOM BRUNEL

CLEAR ROAD AHEAD

Posters. These are all reproductions made from the Posters themselves, and not from my originals.

ROYAL BORDER BRIDGE
BERWICK·ON·TWEED
ON THE EAST COAST ROUTE BETWEEN ENGLAND AND SCOTLAND
BRITISH RAILWAYS

PORT TO PORT
The ships owned and operated by British Railways offer a reliable and regular cross Channel service every day throughout the year

BRITISH RAILWAYS
GIANTS
"PACIFICS" IN THE DON

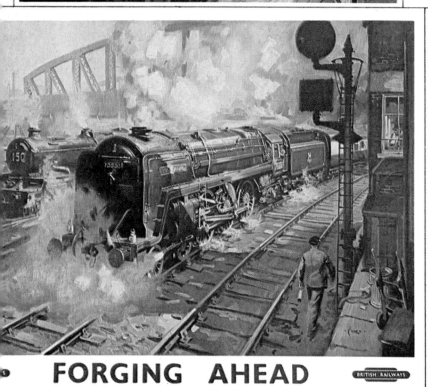

FORGING AHEAD
BRITISH RAILWAYS

DERBY LOCOMOTIVE WORKS
AN ENGINE IS WH
BRITISH RAILWAYS

EFRESHED

ER LOCOMOTIVE WORKS

LED

BRITISH RAILWAYS

GLEN OGLE

PERTHSHIRE

SEE SCOTLAND BY RAIL

BRITISH RAILWAYS

DOLGOCH STATION

27

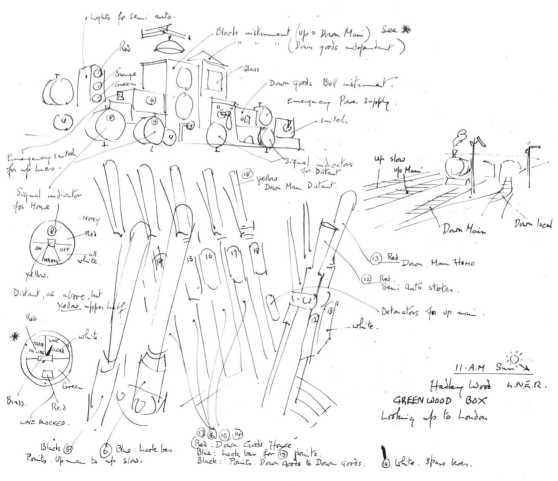

Lights for semi auto.

Red

Orange
Green

Block instrument (up & Down Main)   See *
   "   "   "   (Down goods independant)

Glass

Down goods Bell instrument.

Emergency Power supply

switch

Emergency switch
for up lines.

Signal indicators
for Distant.

Signal indicator
for Home

Ivory

Red

all
white

Yellow.

Distant, as above, but
Yellow upper half.

Red

ON   OFF

WRONG

Red

White.

TRAIN
ON LINE   LINE
CLEAR

Green

Red

LINE BLOCKED.

Brass.

Black (5)
Points. Up main to up slow.

(6) Blue: Lock bar.

(18) Yellow
Down Main Distant.

14   15   16   17   18

13

12

up slow
up Main

Down Main   Down local

(13) Red Down Main HOME

(12) Red
Semi Auto starter.

Detonators for up main.

white.

11.A.M Sun

Hadley Wood   L.N.E.R.
GREEN WOOD BOX
Looking up to London

(17) (16) (15) (14)
Red: Down Goods Home
Blue: Lock bar for (15) points.
Black: Points. Down goods to Down goods.   (14) White. Spare lever.

28

ON EARLY SHIFT. Greenwood Box, LNER main line.
These illustrations indicate the preparatory work necessary
before putting oil on canvas. The colour note at left was
made on site in conjunction with the pencil sketch above.
This process is important when undertaking paintings of a
technical nature, particularly so when you bear in mind that
the work, in poster form, will be seen by millions of people,
many of whom are knowledgeable on the subject and *always*
eager to discover mistakes! (See text page 20).
36" × 45"

lifting a 2-6-4 tank
Locomotive Erecting shops, Derby. (g.R. British R

AN ENGINE IS WHEELED
Notes and details made on the spot for a BR Poster in the
Derby works.

The Royal Border Bridge, Berwich on Tweed, looking North. →

"FEET UP"
E 7473 ON THE ROYAL BORDER BRIDGE,
GOING SOUTH.

TRACK LAYING BY NIGHT
The sketches were made in Wandsworth Station, SR, at two →
in the morning in pouring rain. The colour plate shows the
completed Poster. (See text page 19).
33″ × 45″

32   Sketching from the 'High girders' on the Tay Bridge. The diesel was brought up and posed for me.

THE TAY BRIDGE
Working conditions for this Poster were not comfortable. Winds of nearly forty miles an hour were blowing across the Bridge as I sat sketching on top of the 'High Girders', and after a while the noise began to have a peculiar, mesmeric affect on me. You see, as one sketches, one's head is moving constantly from one's drawing to the view ahead, up and down, up and down and in a wind, this head movement causes a fluctuation in the sound within the ear, resulting in a sharp, monotonous alteration in pitch. After an hour I became strangely dizzy and felt that I was toppling sideways and about to fall off the Bridge. As you see, no ledge or hand-rail up here!
36″ × 45″

33

'THE GREAT MARQUESS'
In Tyseley shed. This locomotive is the property of Viscount
Garnock who wrote the foreword to this book.

Working on a detail from
'The Great Marquess'.

THE LICKEY INCLINE
With regulator set wide and with everything but the grate bars going up through the chimney, No. 5993 hammers her way up the steepest gradient in the country. Incidentally, whilst working on this painting I was taken to Broomsgrove churchyard to view a pair of old tombstones. They stand together in memory of two drivers on the Birmingham & Gloucester Railway, both of whom lost their lives through boiler explosions on the Lickey.
30″ × 40″

'CLUN CASTLE'.
On the Turntable, Tyseley, Birmingham.

NOSTALGIA

No. 931 'Kings Wimbledon'.
The man who commissioned
this painting is here
depicted as the capped
and bare-kneed schoolboy
he was during the war
years when the black
liveried engines of the
Southern Region were
some of R.E.L. Maunsell's
most successful designs
and the most powerful
4–4–0s in Europe.
20" × 24"

STORM OVER SOUTHALL SHED
20" × 26"

'THE RIVER'
Dart Valley Railway. To get the environment I wanted, I rode to the end of the line on this engine, standing on the buffer-beam, and equipped with a whistle. Whenever I saw what looked like an effective piece of scenery, I would blow the whistle, the engine would pull up and I would jump down and assess the view. This procedure went on for most of the day and was highly entertaining!.
20″ × 30″

Castle Class Locomotive emerging from the Severn Tunnel into Wales. 30″ × 40″
National Museum of Wales.

THE BRITANNIA BRIDGE
Robert Stephenson masterpiece.
Opened in 1850 and destroyed
by fire in 1970, (see text
page16).
36" × 45"

A 'KING' AT DAWLISH.
30" × 40"

'CASTLE' ON THE COAST
A childhood memory. Coming back to my home in Cornwall from boarding school I would stand eagerly at the carriage window, waiting for the train to rush out of a certain tunnel west of Dawlish and expose to my delighted gaze the famous 'Old Man Rock' . . . My Rock – the 'hols' had started! Of course the picture had to be in 'Great Western' days, and the engine had to be 'Monmouth Castle' (see page 25) as this was the locomotive I rode whilst making sketches for the poster 'Clear Road Ahead'.
30" × 40"

'THE TUNNEL'
King Richard III was the first locomotive in this class to be fitted with the double chimney.
30" × 40"

'THE CHELTENHAM FLYER'
No. 5069 'Isambard Kingdom Brunel'.
The highest speed achieved by this famous train was on the 30 June 1937 when No. 5039 'Rhuddlan Castle' with 8 coaches reached 95 mph. On 5 June, No. 5006 'Tregenna Castle' did the up journey in 56 min. 47 sec. while engine No. 5005 'Manorbier Castle' hauled 7 carriages from Paddington to Swindon, against a slight gradient, in 60 minutes flat. The world record for a start-to-stop run was pushed up to 81.68 mph and this still remains the British record with steam traction. 25" × 30"

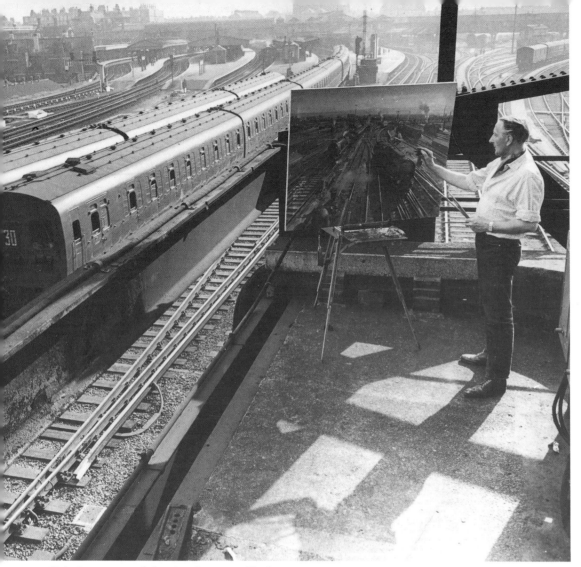

Painting on top of the signal gantry, Clapham.

CLAPHAM JUNCTION

When Don Faulkner, PRO Southern Region, took me on a tour of the Junction to evaluate its merits as a poster subject, I was positively awed and not a little bewildered. Here was a veritable Grand Canyon of railway impedimenta. A vast area of tracks, points and crossovers, signal gantries, bridges and station platforms and out of this tangled medley I had to pick a view which would display the Junction to best advantage. Here is the finished work, but remember, I was faced with a piece of virgin canvas, which meant that before I was in a position to start painting, miles of walking, assessing and rough sketching, all over the site, had to be undertaken. It was only towards the end of the day that, flat-footed and weary, I decided that the long signal gantry, which spanned thirteen tracks, might prove worth a visit. It certainly was! I knew instantly that I had found the spot. From up there I looked down on virtually all the tracks, giving a fine background interest with the lines swinging in graceful complimentary curves to right and left against a misty summer evening sky.

After a preliminary drawing I later took the 38″ × 40″ canvas up on to the gantry and painted a great deal of the subject on the spot. Trains came rattling past in constant procession, to left, to right and slap beneath the spot on which I stood. I indicated several of these whenever I found them occupying positions in accord with my compositional inclinations. But here I realised I could be on dangerous ground. I decided to take professional advice. Entering the signal-box I displayed the canvas. The men crowded around. They appeared delighted and showered me with flattering comment. 'But is there anything wrong with it, technically?' I pleaded. This question abruptly altered the attitude of my audience. The signalmen studied the work in sombre silence, then, 'Look!' said one, in horror, 'He's got a light engine on the same road as the down Portsmouth express will be in a couple o' minutes! Lumme, that won't do, now will it?'

That was just the start of it. They certainly went to work on me and I retired from the box in the gloomy knowledge that all but two of my trains must be painted out and replaced in positions which would not jeopardise the lives of the travelling public.

How many people, I wonder, realise that at certain times of the day over thirty trains can pass this spot, the largest junction in the world, in a *single minute*! Surely a triumph in signal control and organisation.

38″ × 40″

Sketch made on the footplate, at
speed. 'Flying Scotsman'.

WINTER AND THE 'SCOTSMAN'.
30″ × 40″

44

THE FOOTPLATE
Alan Peglar at the controls of his very own locomotive, the
world famous and much travelled 'Flying Scotsman'. To paint
this picture, I had to cram myself tightly into the tender
corridor-doorway, to enable myself to get far enough away to
work. No sort of commission for a fat guy!
30" × 40"

A 'DUCHESS' ON SHAP.
38" × 48"

'THE DUCHESS OF HAMILTON'
The actual 'Duchess' was brought out, freshly painted and
gleaming into the sunlight from inside York Museum to pose
for her portrait. Smoke, steam, landscape and super elevation
were all added, within the comfort of the studio.
36" × 45

← EXPRESS ENGINES AT TYSELEY.
Two old steam 'flyers' that have been preserved and spared
the guillotine of progress. 30″ × 40″

SCOTSMAN ON THE FORTH
The first time the 'Flying Scotsman' ever crossed the Forth
Bridge – I went with her in the cab! On page 17 I attempt to
describe the circumstances of this hectic if somewhat
rumbustious experience.
30″ × 40″

← THE STATION.
'Queen of The Belgians' at New Street, Birmingham.
30″ × 40″

Driving 'King George V' at Hereford.

Working on the Bulmer painting. This photo was taken by a great railway enthusiast and photographer, the late Eric Treacy, Bishop of Wakefield.

A 'KING' AT HEREFORD

The train, with its string of immaculate green and cream coaches, consisting of the vestibule coach, 'Aquilla', built in '51 to commemorate the Festival of Britain, a dining-car, a bar coach, a museum and a cinema coach, is the property of the Bulmer Cider Company. It is drawn by a beautifully renovated Great Western monarch, 'King George V' and sets off periodically from Hereford on a marathon journey of exactly three-quarters of a mile!

I have, on occasions, been privileged to take lunch aboard this singular 'express' and as an excellent meal is being served by monkey-jacketed stewards, the train eases gently away from the station platform and sets off down the line. Then, equally gently it draws up and after a decent pause, reverses and proceeds backwards into the station. This lively sequence, accompanied by a merry jingling of cutlery and glass-ware, is repeated throughout the duration of the meal, until, at due length, when coffee and liqueurs have been leisurely consumed, one steps again on to the platform of Hereford station, both replete and surprisingly fresh after the rigours of this delightful but somewhat eccentric journey. 30″ × 40″

MEMORIES OF WILLESDEN JUNCTION
With cylinder cocks open and roaring, an LMS 'Black Five' begins to move out. I refer to this picture as a memory, as it was here, in the summer of 1937, that I used to drive steam engines. (Unofficially of course!) 30″ × 40″

← PREPARATIONS FOR DEPARTURE
A shed scene offers the most dramatic and intimate association with the steam engine that an artist could wish for and when night closes in, that quality is increased, ten-fold. 30" × 40"

DEPARTURE FROM PADDINGTON
'Hall' class, 5935, pulls out from number two departure platform at Paddington, adding her exhaust steam to the murk of a London winter's morning. Incidently, it was from this very spot, years ago, that I made my studies for the poster, 'Forging Ahead'. (See page 26).
20" × 24"

← OUT OF THE NIGHT
Portrait of a Great Western 'King' (somehow I can never get around to referring to Isambard Kingdom Brunel's mighty enterprise as Western Region.) Anyway, railway or region, these superb engines are among the aristocrats of Britain's Steam Era. 30" × 40"

DOUBLE HEADER IN THE HIGHLANDS
I rode the footplate of many of these fine L.M.S. Class 5's or
'Black Fives' as they were more commonly known, while
making studies for B.R. Posters, on the Oban line, in
Scotland. To hear their thunderous voice pounded up Glen
Ogle, was something to remember. 30″ × 40″

NIGHT EXPRESS
A Southern Railway rebuilt Merchant Navy, No 35027 'Port Line', pounds labourously up Parkstone bank with a heavy night express. 30″ × 40″

First sketch
for the painting,
'Evening Star'

Sketch for "Evening Star"
Southall shed.

AUTUMN OF STEAM

This weatherbeaten class 9F was mine for the day. Her boiler pressure was down but there was steam enough to move her. In solitary state I drove her from the shed at Southall, out on to the turntable and back over two sets of points until I had her, posed against the rust and weeds of a forgotten siding.

This setting I felt was an appropriate epitaph to the last months in the life of a fine old engine. 30″ × 40″

← 'EVENING STAR'

Or, the mouse that nearly caused an international incident. Here is the story, and it's a true one.

When this painting was reproduced as an art print by the firm of James Haworth, a copy, was purchased by an Officer on a Union Castle liner and was hanging in his cabin when the liner docked at Cape Town. The Captain of the ship happened to bring a friend of his, a member of a famous Cavalry Regiment, to this man's cabin for some reason or other. The soldier immediately noticed the print on the wall. 'That's one of Cuneo's, isn't it?' he asked. 'You know, the feller who always paints a mouse in his pictures'. The other two regarded the soldier in some surprise. Neither of them had ever heard of me, nor had they any knowledge of rodents being inserted into oil paintings. Three able-bodied men then approached the print and searched it thoroughly. Not one of them could find the mouse!

Finally, the Captain said, 'Look here, get a cable off to this chap Haworth and tell him for God's sake to let us know where the bloody thing is!' John Haworth senior duly received this graphic request. He thought for a while and then decided, that 'Up telegraph pole first right', constituted both a clear and inexpensive reply. He promptly dispatched this message back to the liner.

It arrived in Cape Town, but instead of being delivered to the ship, it was sent direct to the South African equivalent of MI5, as a highly suspicious message, *probably in code*. Whereupon, two members of the Security Force stomped up the gangway of the British ship and demanded to see the Captain. That good man was in his cabin sitting at his desk. The cable was thrust before him. 'Would you kindly explain this, Sir.'

The Captain took the paper. He goggled at it. He had long forgotten the incident and the words meant nothing to him. 'Up telegraph pole first right.' What in hell did that mean? He hadn't a notion. The Captain rose up, his face reddening in anger, when suddenly he caught sight of the word Haworth and he remembered. 'Gentlemen', he announced with great solemnity, 'Follow me.' He led his visitors down through the ship and finally stopped at his officer's cabin. He flung wide the door and with the air of a conjurer producing a rabbit from a hat, pointed dramatically at the print. 'There you are, gentlemen – Up telegraph pole first right – and THERE'S THE MOUSE!'

30″ × 40″

YESTERDAY'S WINTER. Memories of the footplate, U.S.A. Perhaps all my enthusiasm for the steam engine has gone into this painting. Its power, its weight, its romantic appeal and above all, its warm heart. 44" × 72"

THE MIGHTIEST OF THE MIGHTY
One of the Union Pacific's 'Big Boys' takes on
coal and water at Harriman, Wyoming, before
tackling the heavy grade over the mountain to
Laramie.
These 594 ton locomotives were the largest
and heaviest ever built and could do the work
of four conventional engines. The thunderous
anthem from their exhaust could, on a still
day, be heard eight miles and more away and
when working the 100-plus freight-car 'drags'
up Sherman Hill, a bull-dozer had periodically
to be brought in to clear a track-side clogged
from the hailstorm of cinders that rained
down hot and stinging from the smoke-stack.
To me these 6,000 horse-power giants
represent the ultimate in might and majesty
and for the railroads of America they surely
symbolise the final magnificence in steam
motive power.
Alas, the reign of the 'Big Boy' was to come to
a sad but inevitable close, when, in the
summer of '57, the Union Pacific brought in
the new gas turbines and diesels for use on
the Hill.
The Shire horse had been superseded by – the
tractor
40″ × 50″

MONARCHS OF STEAM
36″ × 45″

'FLÊCHE D'OR'
A 'Chapelon' pulls out of Calais – in the days when the →
station was open to the sky. 30″ × 40″

Making notes for the Calais Poster, 'Bon Voyage'.

← 'BON VOYAGE'

The circumstances of the construction of this B.R. Poster, were bizarre to say the least and not a little tinged with school-boy idiocy on my part! Don Faulkner, of the Southern Region, had taken me over to Calais specially for this preposed, English–French poster theme.

I had been warned that the trains would not remain for long after the boat docked, therefore, immediately the 'Invicta's' gang plank was down and the inevitable flood of garlic-impregnated porters began clambering up it, I tore off, deftly avoiding the Customs, and made a bee-line for the locomotives. The move, however, proved disappointing. I quickly realised a ground level position was useless. I had to get aloft somehow, as that would be the only way in which to embrace both trains and ships in the picture. Somewhere I found a ladder. I grabbed it and assuring an official that I would be but a minute, put it up against the side of a wagon-lits and shinned up to the roof. Once aloft, I scampered around, moving from coach to coach, scribbling madly at compositional notes. Suddenly a whistle blew and the train I was on began to move! I sprinted back along the roofs, jumping the gap between coaches like an Olympic hurdler. The ladder *had gone*! I stuffed the sketch-book inside my shirt, grabbed at a hand-rail, slithered down on to the

buffers and leapt off as the train gathered speed – slap into the arms of a portly gendarme. The man promptly got a stranglehold on me and frog-marched me to the Customs shed. Here, explanations and unpleasantness awaited. My baggage had been impounded and if it had not been for the diplomatic handling of the situation by Don, I may well have landed myself behind bars. However, all was eventually forgiven. I borrowed a bicycle from a long-suffering 'wheel-tapper' and pedalled off, contrite but still brimming with verve, to the loco depot for the required engine details; this time from the vantage point of a cattle-truck's roof, which vehicle I managed to get wheeled into the necessary position.

That night Don and myself slept on board the French steamer, 'Cote d'Azur' (seen in background) but as neither of us could locate any light switches, we did so in total darkness.

The next morning, by dint of more ladder-climbing and sketching from a signal-box and the cab-top of a handy tank-engine, I completed my studies and returned to mother England.

All that need be done now was to sort out the stuff I had gleaned in Calais and simply paint the picture – *dead easy*! 36″ × 45″

← 'SEE, HERE IS A PICTURE OF MY GRANDSON'
A class 230 DI waits in Boulogne depot.
I always feel that these fine engines have a touch of the
greyhound about them. Indeed, owing to their speed
potential, they were affectionately known by their drivers as
the 'Runners'. They certainly had this remarkable ability to
pull away from a standstill with a heavy load behind the
tender, with but the merest whisper of exhaust. A classic
locomotive, a joy to see in motion and a favourite of mine
from childhood.
30″ × 40″

← SUNSET OF AN ERA
Boulogne depot. 30″ × 40″

NIGHT TRAIN TO PARIS
I came upon this by chance whilst on holiday and motoring
down through France to the south. I was enthralled. The
beautiful 'Chapelon' pacific stood dark against the night sky,
framed by the light from the signal-box and the myriad lights
on and around the black silhouette of the gantry. The
painting was built up entirely from the scribbles and
colour-notes I was able to make that night, but for the
detailed know-how of the locomotive I repaired to my
stamping ground, Boulogne depot.
30″ × 40″

THE OPENING OF THE STOCKTON & DARLINGTON RAILWAY

Excitement galore!'Locomotion 1', with George Stephenson at the throttle, slowly but surely draws away from the straining equestrian team she was to to supercede. Before that fateful day in 1825 a good horse was the fastest means of transport in the world.
22" × 28"

THE TURNTABLE

A French Nord engine, class 230 DI, eases forward → off the 'table', at Boulogne, to the accompaniment of hissing steam from open cylinder cocks and the rhythmic thump from her side pump.
25" × 30"

THE MARCH HARE

'THE MAD ENGLISH'

70

← THE MARCH HARE
Here is a little old 'lady' that truly delights me. Note the
drooping buffer-beam and the 'rat-hole' in the chimney. I
should dearly love to own such an engine. I discovered her
and sat quietly sketching her in the yards at Valladolid,
Northern Spain. It was only when the drawing was
transferred to canvas that the little engine leapt into life and
spun her wheels in lively gait.
20″ × 30″

← 'THE MAD ENGLISH'
What inspired me to paint this bedlamite extravaganza was
seeing an ancient wood-burning locomotive chugging
through the Norwegian mountains. I followed her for miles
by car as she careered in and out of tunnels and over
viaducts. On returning to England I'm blessed if I didn't
come across a 1906 Mercedes racer, simply asking to pose.
Then, to top it all I actually found this old 'Crampton' during
the war, puffing about in a goods yard outside Paris, *still*
working!
No doubt some of my readers will notice a similarity in
treatment between this painting and 'Bentley V Blue Train'
Well, why not? Both in spirit and conception they
are virtually identical.
25″ × 30″

LOCOMOTIVES WAITING TO ENTER THE DEPOT
Boulogne. 30″ × 40″

THE PENYDARREN TRAMROAD LOCOMOTIVE.

Trevithick strides beside his engine, whilst a carpenter, saw in hand, watches for any low branches which could foul the chimney or flywheel and thus impede the progress of their fantastic 'iron horse'.

I have attempted to capture the excitement of the occasion on that 22 February 1804 when the locomotive successfully hauled a load of 10 tons of bar-iron and some seventy passengers on the tramroad between the iron-works and a loading point on the Glamorganshire Canal at Abercynon, a distance of nine-and-half-miles. The locomotive – the first ever to draw a load on rails accomplished the journey in four hours and five minutes.

Commissioned for the Department of Industry by the late Mr Richard Trevithick, MICE, great-grandson of the inventor and my personal friend. 25″ × 30″

Study of Trevithick's Penydarren Tramroad Locomotive.

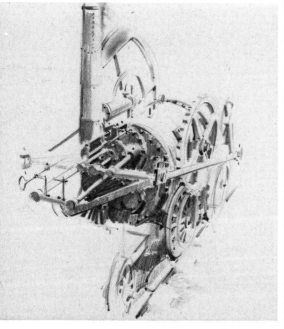

INTO THE '80s.
An allegory, commissioned by the Railways and designed to introduce the new A.P.T. (Advanced Passenger Train) The theme: the future – suring forth in all its fresh, electrical glory, whilst behind – seen dimly, stand the proud ghosts of a dead era. An ordinary enough interpretation perhaps, but nevertheless, one of the most dangerous and hair-raising commissions I ever tackled.
I tell the story as a finale to this book and come to think of it – it could well have proved *mine*!
(See text page 24) 38″ × 40″

RAIN IN THE YARDS

As soon as commitments at Detmold for E. Battery, Royal Horse Artillery were over, I set off for the nearest smell of hot oil, steam and coal dust. At Rheine Locomotive depot, north of Munster and twenty-five miles East of the Dutch Border, I found all I wanted – in pelting rain! However, a co-operative Battery Commander and his umbrella made sketching possible. 20″ × 24″

← Study of the 'Flêche d'Or'.

77

THE VOICE OF THE GIANT
Freight train, West Germany.
30" × 40"

THE SOLE SURVIVOR
I discovered this veteran tucked into a corner of Soltau Shed, West Germany. The actual purpose of the visit was to see the unveiling of my painting of the Battle of Sidi Rezegh, for the 7th Armoured Brigade and this engine 'find', was a pure bonus. She stood there towering above me; run down, rusty and forlorn – but somehow magnificent still.
30″ × 40″

CAME THE DIESELS.
This old engine, put 'out to rust' on track scarcely longer than itself, stands a lonely memorial to the steam era on the salt flats of Formanterra, Ibiza. 30″ × 40″

NIGHT TRAIN TO MOMBASA
East African Railways. 24″ × 40″

PORTRAIT OF A FIREMAN
Cape Town Shed.
24″ × 20″

THE PASS TRACK. High in the mountains of Northern Ethiopia →
a little Italian 'Mallet' slogs its way up from the Red Sea to Asmara. 20″ × 24″

ATMOSPHERE OF STEAM
Beneath a back-drop of Table Mountain, the running sheds
of Cape Town, South Africa.
20" × 40"

MAINTENANCE ON SHED IN THE '50s
In the days of my early visits to South Africa and Rhodesia, locomotives carried one big head-lamp on the boiler-front, unlike the smaller, double-lensed, boxed-in pair they are equipped with today. It was a 'Garratt' like the one here, that I rode on through the night, coming down from the Victoria Falls to Bullawayo. I was struck then, by the brilliance that one great lamp shed along the track ahead. (See text page 15).
25" × 30"

← FREIGHT EAST FROM PIETERMARITZBURG
A class GMAs 'Garratt' fills the darkening sky with her steam and her smoke as she stomps across the South African veldt. Note the tank-car for additional water, hitched behind the engine; a familiar sight with nearly every 'Garratt'.
30" × 40"

85

← THE ORE TRAIN
A Tank locomotive working on a Gold Mine outside
Johannesburg.
Note the picturesque old wooden head-gear, now alas, like
the steam engine itself, gone forever.
25″ × 30″

THE LAST STEAM LOCOMOTIVE TO WORK IN MALAYSIA
This old British built engine No. 564.36 has been presented
to the indigenous Indian population. She will be used once a
year, to take passengers up to the 'Thaipusam' festival at the
temple of the Batu caves, but will still be kept and maintained
at Bangsar shed, Kuala Lumpur, where I painted her.
25″ × 30″

← AQUA CALDA – ON ROUTE TO THE RED SEA
A train pulls in to a village halt and immediately a flock of
women dash towards the locomotive. Mystified by this
behaviour, I soon discovered the reason for it. They were on
the scrounge for hot water for the household! It appears to
be the thing on these halts for a driver to allow villagers to
fill the odd pot, can or jug direct from the boiler of his
engine. 24″ × 40″

87

THE LEVEL CROSSING,
BARRACKPORE, INDIA.
The lavish use of silver paint on
boiler and smoke box is characteristic.
Note, too, the situation! Such an
eventuality could hold up a train
indefinitely, in India. (see text page
16). 38″ × 48″

STABLING FOR THE LITTLE GIANTS
This cute little railway is both an institution and a delight.
Like the Cable-car that winds its angled way from Market
Street to Fisherman's Wharf in San Francisco, the Darjeeling
Railway of India represents a symbolism that must never be
allowed to pass from us. I pray that good common sense may
prevail and that we act in time to assure the continuing
presence of these priceless gems of yesterday. However, there
is already a rumour of an endangered Cable-car and I have
seen a *diesel* at Darjeeling!
20″ × 30″

THE OLD RED CABOOSE

Albert Canyon, Canadian Pacific Railway. Here is a place in which I formed tranquility – Albert Canyon in the heart of the Canadian Rockies, where the stillness and silence seem absolute.

At the time I discovered this lovely spot I was painting a scene of the building of the Trans-Canada highway up in the mountains above Revelstoke. I particularly remember the commission as I had to pose the entire earth-moving equipment of the operation one Friday evening before the work crew went for the weekend. I was then left on my own until the following Tuesday morning (Monday being Victoria Day and a holiday) to work on my subject. I was given a truck, and used to drive myself to and from the site along a rock-strewn road where anything over 5 miles-an-hour was enough to dislocate one's spine, and then clamber up the mountain, humping easel, paints, canvas and a lunch bag.

For three days I saw not a soul; in fact, my only companions were black bears, and my only fear that one of them might turn out to be a Grizzly!

Way below me across the river ran the tiny thread of the CPR main line, and occasionally I would hear the 'trumpet' of a diesel and pause to watch the long red freight wind its way through the mountains. 28" × 30"

NORTHBOUND FREIGHT
Canadian National Railway
I travelled for miles on the footplate of this great C.N.R. →
diesel with the thermometer registering 38° below. Beneath us, dark against the snow and snaking away into the far haze, the ribbon of steel transporting us to Thompson, Churchill and Hudson Bay. 28" × 30"

TO RUSSIA, WITH LOVE

Mail from home being unloaded near Archangel for men of the British Army of Occupation in Russia, 1919.

Of the set of six paintings that hang in the Officers Mess of the Royal Engineers barracks at Mill Hill, depicting the Army Postal and Courier Service, this is the subject I enjoyed most. The research for it was quite something – Russian and British First World War Uniforms; the type of shaggy little pony the Russians used and the harness, with that decorative and characteristic 'arch' above the horse; station buildings, wagons and, of course, the locomotive. I learnt that at this time (1919) and earlier, Russian engines enjoyed a wealth of individual expression both in colour and design. Indeed, it was not unknown to see a bright pink locomotive in service, apart from those painted in greens, browns and scarlet, whilst some even boasted a portrait of Lenin, on the tender! Wheels, too, were brilliantly coloured and engines often lined-out with ornate extravagence. My engine, I fear, does not support these kaleidoscopic indulgences, she is a mere

work-horse, but nevertheless, displays a feature which has always intrigued me about Russian locomotives – the ship-like hand-rail which encompasses boiler from cab-side to buffer-beam.

I delved and discovered the reason. Years ago, it seems, a fireman fell from a moving locomotive and was killed. The Tsar, apparently upset by the tragedy, ordered that in future every engine should be equipped with a stout double rail fixed around all running-boards to avoid any future possibility of unnecessary loss of life. The custom has remained in the Soviet Union ever since.
48" × 60"

'VOLTAGE VERSUS STEAM'

Owing to a sporting chance of getting oneself electrocuted →
from overhead high-voltage wires, I was forbidden access to an elevated platform from which to work. The only alternative, a nearby bridge where my models – both steam and electric – were brought up into the required pose, beneath it. 40" × 30"

GROOMING THE DIESELS.
Locomotive Shed outside Kings Cross. 40″ × 30″

George Stephenson at the throttle of 'Locomotion 1'. Drawing, for the painting, 'The opening of the Stockton and Darlington Railway, 1825'.

"THE ROCKET

BURY LOCOMOTIVE, LONDON & BIRMINGHAM RLY 1840.

:285

Most brilliant light. COPPER
warm

BRASS

Rivets wider
spaced at rear
of smoke box

whistle

Boiler water
level cocks.

BRASS
safety valve.

Cooler
Light.

Brass

Black

Brass
explain

COMET

4 links

Lined in black red edged

Brass

railing wheel
ater than 1840!

Drivers 4 feet

Buffer beam
as boiler.

wood

Brass splashers

steel.

Bright steel.

← 'The Rocket', as she appeared at the time
of the Rainhill Trials, 1829.

99

Pale cobalt green shutters. **Note:** To close door windows, these shutters
white roof edged with black.

Black; as <u>all</u> handrails on coach

Black.

2nd CLASS MANCHESTER & LEEDS . RLY
Height from floor to roof 6'.

Black.

Olive green from here down.
Each panel thus

Light wood.

3RD CLASS
LONDON

railway

2 l

in gold.

SECOND
CLASS

Bright red.

In gold letters on
each door.

bright
stripe.

Brass

Olive green

'Crampton' locomotive. Drawing made from a model
in the Science Museum, London.

Derby locomotive erecting shop. →

uld be
hand rear
e sketch is used.

Guiding sparks.

2-6-4 Vault on the Crane.

'The Great Marquess', Tyseley, Birmingham.

'Duchess of Hamilton', sketched outside York Museum.

THE DUCHESS OF HAMILTON
No. 46229

'The strippers', Derby. →

"THE STRIPPERS"
Derby Locomotive Shops

French Yard.

"See, here is picture of my grandson"

S.N.C.F.
230 D 1.

Class known by
drivers as the "Runners"

Details for painting, 'See, here is a picture of my Grandson' (see page 68).

Detail, made from roof
of cattle-truck, for Poster,
'Bon Voyage' (see page 66).

Calais
"Bon Voyage"

On the footplate
of the Paris Lyons Express.
May 3rd 1940

The fireman watching the
gauges, inbetween shovelling coal.

Etat, 4-6-2 locomotive
on the way down to Grenoble at night,
Illustrated London News French Armament Factory tour.

"The hospital train"
American S.160.

← 'The fireman'. Sketch made at speed
on Paris Lyon night express, 1940.

American built class S.160,
heading a hospital train, 1944.

United States s.160 loco unloaded.
on to French soil, 1944

United States Army S.160, unloaded
onto French soil during the war.

sky very war[m]

Loco purplish grey.

Dirty india red.

indian

war house

Blue green light

Iron.

Pale crossing wood grey

ye

Pale rust

SAINT LUKE YARDS
MONTREAL.

'Saint Luke Yards', C.P.R. Montreal.
Rough sketch for painting.

CHIHUAHUA,
MEXICO. 1960

Train passing through a street, Chihuahua, Mexico, 1960.

Outside Barrackpore station, India.

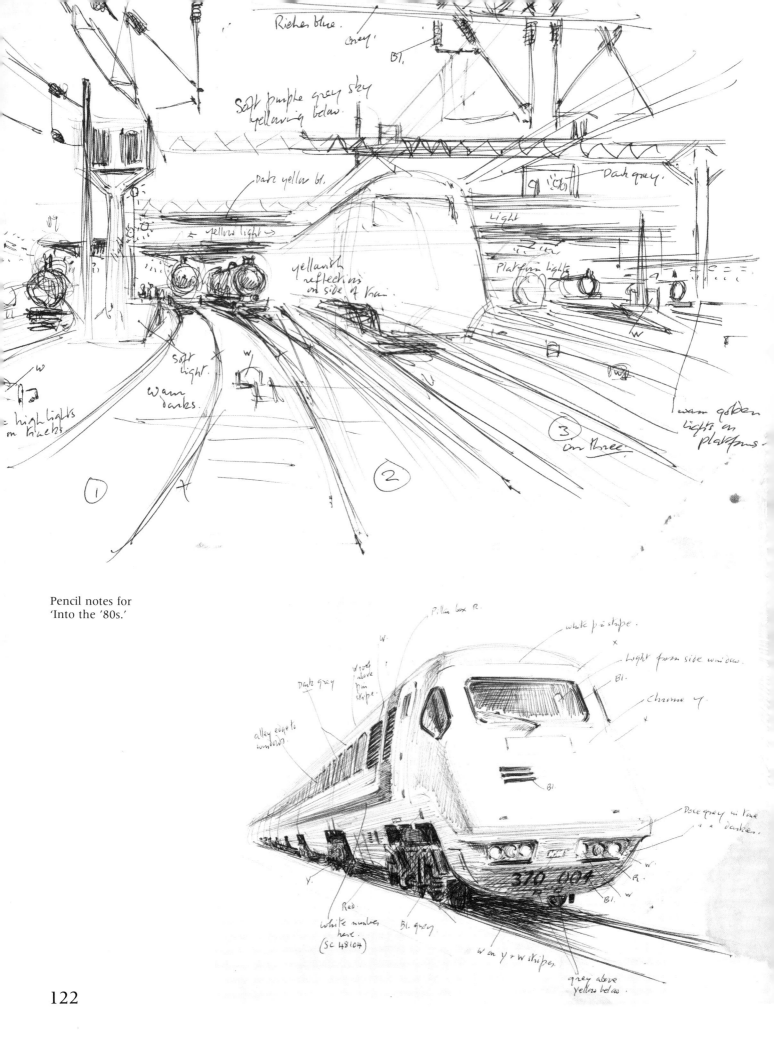

Riches blue.

grey

Bl.

Soft purple grey sky
yellowing below.

Dark grey.

Dark yellow bl.

Light

yellow light →

Platform lights

yellowish
reflections
on side of train.

Soft
light.

Warm
darks.

W

warm golden
lights on
platforms.

highlights
on tracks

W

③
on three

①

✗

②

Pencil notes for
'Into the '80s.'

Pillar box R.

white p stripe.

W.

✗

Light from side windows

Work
above
Pin
stripe.

Dark grey

Bl.

Chrome y.

✗

alloy edge to
windows.

Dove grey in tone
- darker.

W.
R.

Y.

Bl.
W

Red

white number
here
(SC 48104)

Bl. grey

W on y + w stripes.

370 004

grey above
yellow below.

122

First compositional rough for, 'Into the '80s'.

First compositional
"rough" for the Euston Posters
INTO THE 80s.

Glossary of Paintings and sketches

Index

BIBLIOGRAPHY

The Studio   from 1950s
Art & Industry   from 1950s
The Artist   1950s to 1970s
Illustrated London News   from 1939
War Illustrated 1939 to 1945
The Soldier   from 1943
Courier   1950s to 1960s
The Strand   1950s to 1960s
The Railway Magazine   from 1970s
Steam Age   from 1970s
The Field   1975
Hearth & Home   1970
Visual   1963
Transport Age   1960s to 1980s

THE MOUSE & HIS MASTER
The life and work of Terence Cuneo.
New Cavendish Books 1977

ON SHED
Darjeeling Railway, October 1981.